STOP THINKING NEGATIVELY

(How to manage your mind and be in control of what you think)

BY

DOUGLAS WRIGHT

Table of content

Chapter 1

Take charge of your self-talk and reframe your internal dialogue.

Simply put, your "inner dialogue" is made up of your thoughts. That internal voice offers conscious and unconscious commentary on your life.
Do you ever catch yourself talking to yourself? What are the persistent ideas that run through your mind?

Whether you're aware of it or not, you may utilize your inner dialogue as a potent instrument to create the life you want. Your inner voice guides every decision you make, so pay attention to what it has to say.

But what if you want to change the way your inner voice is phrased? If you regularly think negatively, you already know that it can become a self-fulfilling prophecy. You are less likely to project confidence and accomplish your goals if you think and speak negatively more often. More significantly, if you can't think positively, you can't live the life you want.

Instead of getting caught up in the thoughts or feelings of others, start by just paying attention to how you feel about something.

The various voices we hear in our heads

The three types of critical thoughts we have about ourselves are self-doubt, self-judgment, and self-criticism. It's important to recognize how you speak to yourself since the various voices in your head can be a major distraction.

SELF DOUBT

All of us have been there. We all experience times in our life when we wonder if we are doing enough or if we are strong enough to handle all the uncertainties that can arise as we age. We may feel self-conscious about the choices and decisions we've made, or we just think we're not good enough. When we lack confidence or believe we are unable to do tasks, we experience self-doubt. People who doubt themselves worry about things not going as planned or are uncertain about things they can't control.

A certain amount of self-doubt is beneficial since it shows that you are aware of your shortcomings. However, ongoing anxiety and self-doubt can negatively impact your life greatly.

How doubting yourself keeps you stuck

Imagine that your manager believes you are the best candidate in the room and has given you a crucial responsibility. But instead of seeing it as a compliment on your job, you begin to worry.

You worry that you won't be able to perform well. You worry that it will be widely ridiculed at work if you don't do it effectively. You spend a lot of time worrying about every choice you make and imagining what might go wrong.

It is expected that terror will then play a significant part in your small drama. You become more prone to putting things off. You put off doing your work and lack motivation.
After the story, you submit your work at the last minute, and you will feel as though "I can do more than this."

Common Causes of Self-Doubt

There are several causes for self-doubt. Here, we'll go over a few of them.

1. Previous mistakes and experience

Past experiences, particularly negative ones like being in an abusive relationship or getting fired without a valid reason, can have a significant impact on how we respond. In these circumstances, our mental health may suffer greatly.

Our beliefs can be rattled and shaken by the experience. But continuing to draw on the past without learning from it is a waste of your promising future!

2. Childhood upbringing

Our behaviors and personalities are significantly influenced by our upbringing. You may already have adopted the habit of questioning if your parents repeatedly told you that you weren't good enough or if you attended a school where pupils' grades were strongly weighted. You may have already developed the habit of self-reflection.

3. Comparing Yourself to Others

We live in a competitive environment, so comparing ourselves to others is not out of the ordinary for us.

With coworkers or just the vast world of social media, it is simple to compare our work performance. It's simple for us to feel inferior to others and envious of their lives.

You'll start to lose yourself if you constantly judge others by what they have and what you don't.

4. New Challenges

Given that we have no prior experience with this situation, this is a rather typical one. Uncertainty and insecurity will make you feel uncomfortable.

5. Fear of Failure / Fear of Success

Should you take a chance should you play it safe? Whether you want to ask someone on a date or run a marathon, there are both potential risks and rewards. Logically you know that if you don't try anything, you also don't gain anything. So, what's holding you back from achieving your goals and living your dreams? It may be fear of failure or fear of success or both. That's right, it's possible to have a fear of failure and a fear of success at the same time.

Fear of failure is pretty straightforward. No one wants to put in effort only to have their project tank or plans fall through. Even worse, no one wants to feel like s/he is a failure.

How to Get Rid of Self-Doubt

What can you do to get over self-doubt and regain confidence despite the challenges you face?

1. Get on your feet and exclaim "Stop"!

When you become aware of the negative thoughts you are having, make an effort to remain in the present and concentrate on the good.

Try to have something upbeat ready that you may turn to if you feel down or uncertain of yourself. Ideas for what to prepare to include:

a list of refutations, such as "I can accomplish this" and "It's just another opportunity for me to learn,"
a jar filled with pleasant memories
a collection of all the images that bring you joy
a list of simple exercises you may take to increase your energy
a package of wholesome snacks you can

2. Break for a Moment to Recharge Your Optimism

Sometimes it becomes more difficult for us to emerge from a circumstance or emotion the longer we feel stuck in it.
Just unwind for a while and change your attention to something else. By doing this, we can free up our thoughts and adopt a brand-new viewpoint.

Try making a list of things for which you are thankful if you need to increase your optimism. Your thinking will automatically change for the better as a result of this.

The most effective predictor of well-being, according to one study measuring gratitude, hope, optimism, and life satisfaction, was gratitude. That's a pretty good reason to cultivate gratitude, right?

3. Never Be Afraid to Ask for Help

While improving oneself is crucial, it's also a good idea to enlist the help of your loved ones, such as family and friends. Ask for assistance without hesitation.

They might be your spouse, your parents, your siblings, your friends, your mentors, your boss, or even a coach.

It can also boost our self-confidence and keep us motivated to get guidance and confirmation from others.

Final Remarks

It's normal for us to have doubts about ourselves, but you must realize that if you panic and remain trapped for too long, nothing good will come of it. As soon as you can, try to break out of the crowd and put effort into developing your own identity. You do not have to be held back by self-doubt.

SELF JUDGMENT

Every day, we pass judgment. It's in our instinct to assume the worst or form prejudices. Whether we are aware of it or not, we make them about ourselves as well as about other people. Simple is the definition. We form opinions about ourselves that we refer to as self-judgments.

I don't have a flat enough stomach.
I'm not intelligent enough.
"I don't deserve to be loved or respected," she said.
"I'm too (insert another arbitrary, critical self-assessment here)."

It might be challenging to stop once you start listening to your harsh self-talk. Your capacity to view yourself favorably can deteriorate. You may eventually begin to accept these things to the point where they become fundamental ideas about who you are. The next step is that you'll probably start unwittingly focusing more on the aspects of your life that serve as support for these unfavorable ideas.

Consider the phrase "I'm not smart enough" as an example.

I think we've all experienced this at some point. It seems sensible that you'd think that. Now imagine that after studying for a test, you didn't perform as well as you had hoped. What follows typically in thoughts? What's wrong with me, you ask? Why didn't I succeed? I must be a moron since I studied. The list is endless. You can use all of this—and most likely will—to bolster your belief that your intelligence is inadequate.

You probably have adequate intelligence. You took an exam and answered numerous questions—some of which were intended to confuse you—while crammed between classmates in an uncomfortable chair and at an uncomfortable temperature, and you didn't perform as well as you had anticipated. Now, I'm not saying tests aren't significant or that you should disregard a subpar grade. I'm trying to emphasize that none of those things about you define you.

Your intelligence cannot be determined by a single test. Your level of beauty is not determined by the form of your stomach. And you deserve to be treated with love and respect, regardless of what you've gone through or what anyone tells you.

Be mindful of your ideas. They frequently become apparent through the way you conduct yourself and how you treat others. Recognize when you are beginning to judge yourself negatively and stop yourself.
Try to instantly make it into a positive thought if you can. If you are unable to make it positive, try making it realistic. I failed one test, which is a more upbeat idea than "I'm not smart enough. I'll take some time to determine what went wrong, fix it, and perform better in the subsequent test.

How to Determine Whether Your Internal Dialogue Is Healthy

Everyone has an inner voice that occasionally guides them through life. Unfortunately, when we do not feel good about who we are and what has occurred to us, this internal speaker may occasionally be destructive, critical, or judgemental of ourselves.

Your self-talk starts to become harmful When:

- You continuously criticize yourself or tear yourself down.
- You are solely considering the drawbacks of a circumstance.

- You hold negative comparisons between yourself and others.
- Your focus is on previous mistakes or failures.
- You keep thinking about a shameful or unpleasant incident.

Here are 3 easy steps you can take to start rephrasing your inner conversation right away.

1. Work on your self-awareness

Without first being aware of it, you cannot alter a condition or modify a habit. Self-awareness is the conscious understanding of one's emotions, personality, and motivations. By engaging in as much awareness practice as you can, you can better comprehend who you are and how you behave.

It matters a lot how you speak to yourself, even if you aren't even aware of it. If you are your own harshest critic, you undoubtedly spend a lot of time overanalyzing and evaluating yourself. Or you might draw the worst possible inference.

You must first recognize the issue to change this habit. From there, you might establish objectives to gradually change the way you talk to yourself. Self-awareness will come to you more readily as you exercise it more frequently. Your overall emotional intelligence will eventually increase as you become more aware of your feelings.

2. Avoid using absolutes

Do you ever catch yourself using phrases like "always" and "never" when you mean something? These words stifle your thinking by placing your ideas in boxes without providing them with the necessary breathing space.

Absolute statements are frequently untrue and do not apply to the truth. You may tell yourself falsehoods like "never" sending emails on time or "always" forgetting to set your alarm in the morning. Rarely does someone act a certain way always or never? It's crucial to refrain from thinking in terms of these claims because they are untrue and can cause you to have unfavorable ideas. It's an excessive all-or-nothing mindset that makes it challenging to advance and adopt a positive outlook.

3. Establish Sound Boundaries

It's critical to comprehend the source of any negative self-talk you engage in. This enables you to make the necessary adjustments to your relationships and environment so that you can have a fulfilling life.

Setting appropriate limits for both yourself and those around you is essential. Dealing with exhausting people and circumstances constantly will make you feel overwhelmed and sad. Additionally, it will result in continuing negative mental patterns.

Get used to saying "no" and not giving unnecessary explanations. Remove it from your life if it causes you more distress than it does happiness. Recognizing your social media usage is also beneficial because it has a significant impact on your inner conversation. Unfollow those who make you sad or who have no use for your time.

Over to You

These suggestions will assist you in beginning to alter your inner dialogue. To ensure that your thought patterns lead you to a healthy, happy existence, paying attention to them is a game-changer. If you don't, you can catch yourself perpetuating bad habits that last much longer than they should.

Chapter 2

Get rid of the tendency of thinking negatively

Most people occasionally battle with overthinking, unfavorable ideas, and worrying. Some people may experience anxiety, pessimism, and depression as a

result of these persistent thought patterns since they feel intrusive and take on a life of their own.
Even while it might not be feasible to stop thinking negatively, it's vital to keep in mind that by cultivating attentive awareness and constructive thought patterns, you can gain control over your ideas and, as a result, manage your emotions and feelings.

Do you ever anticipate a negative outcome before it happens? What causes that to occur?

It's most likely a result of the idea of a self-fulfilling prophecy. A forecast that is destined to come true as a result of the actions that its expression triggers are known as a self-fulfilling prophecy. In essence, your outcome is determined by the way you think. likely, don't go well if you think they won't.

Some people tend to develop the habit of foreseeing the worst-case scenario for themselves. Some people might question why they should bother discussing their thoughts with their supervisor because they believe she is incompetent. "Jenny appears to like Julie more than I do," etc. They're going to become great friends and ignore me, I'm certain of it. The exact thing that was prophesied happens since the person has expended energy worrying and thinking about the dreaded outcome.

They may not always be able to foretell the future. Instead, they unconsciously control their actions with their negative thoughts. People who are afraid to speak up let people talk over them or hold back on ideas, which makes them doubt if they have what it takes to succeed. When someone is afraid of being abandoned by friends, they withdraw from others because they believe they are no longer wanted. Emotions, not facts, are what drive the behaviors. This could develop into a bad habit, an unending chain of unfavorable ideas that results in the negative expected results.

Being your own worst critic is an expression that we have all likely heard. Most likely, we've all had the same experience. Negative self-talk, that critical inner voice that interjects with a message of doubt, fear, blame, or judgment, affects even the most prosperous and content individuals.

Our mental health may be badly impacted if this occurs too frequently. Even if what we're telling ourselves is false, we start to believe it. We may talk ourselves out of pursuing our objectives or relishing

in life's positive moments due to this persistent negative self-talk.
Realizing that we cannot control our thoughts is the first step in stopping negative self-talk. It's not feasible.

The mind will always be thinking. But we can alter the way we speak to ourselves. Meditation can assist in retraining the mind to cease blatantly believing every unfavorable thought and challenging emotion we experience. With this new perspective, we may change our negative self-talk to loving and caring self-talk, boost our self-esteem, and channel our energy towards doing what makes us happy rather than putting ourselves down.

The four basic causes of negative thought patterns.

1 . Monkey Mind

Buddhists refer to this phenomenon as having a monkey mind, where your thoughts wander, swinging from branch to branch. It's all the mental chitchat that you frequently don't even realize is going on. Because of your brain's negativity bias, when you don't check these stray thoughts, they "naturally" skew negative. You cannot continue to engage in thinking about regrets, critiques, and judgments, or worrying about the future.

2. Momentum

Where would you want to stop a car if you were at the top of a steep hill and the brakes failed, causing the car to start rolling down the slope? Which would you prefer—to halt it at the top of the hill or the bottom of the hill?

It's not a ruse, either. You are aware that you would fail terribly and be crushed if you attempted to stop the automobile at the foot of the hill. The car should come to a stop as close to the hill's summit as you can.

However, why is there a distinction? The car is the same and weighs the same at the top and bottom of the hill. It hasn't had a chance to pick up any momentum, so you want to halt it at the top. You are crushed under the tires by the momentum and the force that the motion produces.

The same holds for your thinking. The issue is letting bad thoughts continue to grow throughout the day. Stopping those negative ideas as soon as they arise is the key. If you let them get up to speed, it will be nearly impossible to stop them.

3. It's a Bad habit

The habit of thinking negatively is another possibility. You tend to let your thoughts stray while taking a shower. You frequently daydream while driving. You don't regularly check in with yourself and practice mindfulness in your moments.

These routines take on a life of their own. We allow these outdated cassettes to play continuously and, even though they may not always reflect the truth, we accept them as fact since they have been around for such a long time.

I am unable to find a good dude. I'm terrible at math. Then, our reticular activating system (RAS) assumes control and continuously feeds us evidence supporting these ideas. Anything that doesn't align with these beliefs is also being filtered out by the RAS. As a result, when a good man does appear, you don't see him!

4. You Desire to Be Right

Yup. You'll often compromise your happiness to be correct. When you and your partner are disagreeing, you tell yourself, "But I'm right!" As a result, you refuse to concede, replaying the exchange in your thoughts over and over while growing angrier and angrier over what transpired.

You feel pushed to be correct about something rather than concentrating on being productive, and I refer to this as Correct or Effective. As you try to defend your argument and disprove your spouse, this brings negative ideas and emotions to the fore.

The Three Ineffective Methods for Dealing with Negative Emotions

There are three basic approaches that people typically use to deal with their unfavorable thoughts and feelings.

1. Emotional Snuggies: You might occasionally wrap yourself in an emotional snuggle, as I like to call them. You become so consumed with wanting to be right or wanting to avoid being let down that you encircle yourself in your pessimistic emotions, which begin to feel far too comfortable. You become deeply rooted in these ideas and emotions and forbid yourself from considering anything else. This massive defense mechanism is doing you harm.

2. Ignore them: Hiding your negative emotions or stuffing them doesn't help because others can tell when you're upset even when you're not admitting it, upsetting or stressing them.
Another issue with trying to suppress unpleasant thoughts is that you might be directing your bad emotions in the incorrect direction. This is what we mean when we say that when you are upset with your job, you come home and yell at your child.

Additionally, we are aware that the more effort you put into ignoring something, the more difficult it is to do so (like if I told you right now not to think about a black cat).

3. Ruminating: Continuously thinking about your emotions is the opposite of stuffing them.
Ruminating causes you to revisit events, actions, and emotions, which pushes you farther and further into unfavorable sentiments and thoughts.
You probably start to think, "I'm such an idiot!" Why do I always do this? "Why is it that I can never Y?" You compare yourself to others or some unattainable perfect ideal and end up feeling more nervous or unhappy as a result.

You should put more emphasis on these effective coping mechanisms rather than the ineffective ones: You should use resources to accept, observe, and remove yourself.

How to effectively deal with negative thinking

1. Have a mantra.

A mantra is simply your default phrase or term that will assist you to stop the car's forward momentum as it climbs the slope. You want to be aware of that unfavorable idea and return as quickly as you can to more positive sentiment.

Generally speaking, sayings like "This too shall pass," "This could happen to anyone," or "One day at a time" are effective mantras.

You might also repeat to yourself, "Breath" or "I'm OK right now," as your mantra. I often have a different motto depending on where I am. My motto when I'm with my family is frequently "Love them anyway." Or, "They're making the best use of the resources at hand."

Your mantra could be a prayer, a saying, or pretty much anything that calms you for even a brief time and brings your thoughts into the present.

2. Try to be nice.

One of the simplest methods to get rid of bad thoughts and feelings is to do something pleasant for someone else. When you do that, you get perspective, and it invariably prompts fresh ideas and feelings. When we are kind or generous, it's difficult not to feel better.

3. Ask yourself, "Really?!"

Are you extrapolating all the potential future events from a single current event? "I don't have a job, I'm going to spend all of my savings, and I'm going to end up in a box under the highway!" Really? Are you certain that will occur? You don't have a family member who would first take you in? You don't have any other opportunities or prospects that might present themselves, do you?

What-if scenarios can lead us astray and cause a runaway negative thinking train.

In situations like this, you almost need to bitch slap yourself. Will this one negative event have an impact on the rest of your day, life, or future? Which evidence do you have? Have you ever found yourself living in a box under a bridge, i.e., has this ever occurred to you before? Why wouldn't you be able to do that again even if you have previously pulled yourself out of it?).

It's crucial to keep the incident separate from your entire life and avoid generalizing or catastrophizing.

Speaking to oneself as a friend

Consider how you would act if your best friend were the one experiencing this as a technique to help you distance yourself. What advice would you provide to anyone else in your shoes? Would you treat them with the same severity that you treat yourself?

If you fully simulate talking to them and having a conversation, you'll notice that your language dramatically changes.

4. Distinguish Yourself from the Thought

A tried-and-true method for success is to name the notion and then put some space between yourself and it.

You would therefore adjust your internal monologue from "I'm a bad father" to "I'm having the notion that I'm a bad father."

You can name the emotion as well to give another complexity. When you verbalize your emotions, they lose some of their impacts. You would change "I'll never succeed" to "I'm experiencing the sense of humiliation over this thinking that I'll never succeed."

5. Pay attention to how you are interacting with your negative thoughts:

What do you do when you have negative ideas about yourself? You may already believe them to be true and develop a fixation on such unfavorable concepts. Instead, become aware of your ideas and let them go. Give negative thoughts room to enter, stay, and then leave your mind. Don't hold onto them.

6. Recognize how your thoughts influence your behavior:

Your thoughts and mindset have tremendous power. Your thoughts affect how you behave, and how you behave affects how other people react to you. You're more likely to get what you expect if you approach a situation expecting the worst. Be optimistic that everything will turn out well.

7. Maintain a positive outlook and an open mind: Be assured when approaching any situation and think positively. Keep an open mind to all opportunities and pleasant surprises. Tell yourself that something positive might occur; altering your thoughts can also alter your feelings. A situation has a better chance of succeeding if you get off to the appropriate start.

Avoid adopting an "I told you so" mentality. By being more self-aware, you can change your thinking and break the cycle of unfavorable results and self-fulfilling predictions. You may make your good thoughts come true by thinking positively and resisting the urge to let negative thoughts control you. The next chapter in your life is one that you will write, so make it a happy one!

Chapter 3

Control Your Thoughts and Be the Master of Your Mind

Your perception and, by extension, how you interpret the world are both influenced by your mind, more especially your thoughts.

I've read that the typical human has 70,000 ideas every day. That's a lot, particularly if they are ineffective, abusive toward themselves, or just an overall waste of energy.

You can let your mind wander, but why would you want to? Isn't it time you reclaimed control over your mind and your thoughts? Isn't it time you took the reins?

Decide to ponder your thoughts intentionally and actively. Become someone who has mental control; learn to master your mind.

Changes to your thinking will also result in changes to your feelings, as well as the triggers that cause those sensations.

You feel more at peace knowing that both of these things happened.

There are a couple of thoughts I'm having right now that I didn't choose or that came as a result of my reprogramming. My mind is at peace right now because I am in control of it. Yours could also be

Is Anyone Thinking My Thoughts?

Before you can take control of your thoughts, you must accept that there are some unwelcome "squatters" who are now living in your mind and controlling them.

To rule over them and expel them, you must first understand who they are and why they are doing what they are doing.

Here are four of the "squatters" in your mind who produce harmful ideas.

1. The Inner Critic

This is your ongoing abuser, who frequently consists of:

The opinions of others, frequently your parents

thoughts that you have formed based on your expectations or those of other people

comparing yourself to others, particularly celebrities and public figures

the lies you tell yourself after unpleasant events like betrayal and disappointment. Your perception gives rise to your self-doubt and self-blame, which in situations of rejection and betrayal are probably unfair.

Pain, low self-esteem, a lack of self-acceptance, and a lack of self-love are the Inner Critic's driving forces.
Why else would this individual harm you? Why else would you abuse yourself if this person is you? Why would you allow someone to abuse you in this manner?

2. The Worrier
This individual resides in the hypothetical future.

Fear, which is often unreasonable and unfounded, is what drives the Worrier. Sometimes, this person acts out of dread that what happened in the past will happen again.

3. The Reactor or Troublemaker
This is the one that makes people angry, frustrated, and hurt. These set-offs result from old wounds that haven't fully healed. He will become agitated by any event that is even vaguely connected to a previous injury.
This person can be triggered by thoughts, emotions, sounds, smells, or even words.

The Reactor lacks true motivation and has inadequate impulse control. He is still controlled by old programming that, if it ever did, does not serve you anymore.

4. The Sleep Deprived

This can be a combination of any number of different squatters, including the inner worrier, inner critic, inner planner, and inner ruminator.

Sleep-Deprived may have one of the following motives:

Taking care of the business you ignored throughout the day As a response to silence, which he struggles against Doubt, low self-esteem, uncertainty, and generalized anxiety

As previously mentioned for the inner critic and worrier

How do you keep these squatters under control?

How to Control Your Mind

Both the thinker and the observer of your thoughts are you. You can control your thoughts, but you must be aware of them to determine "who" is in charge of them. Based on this, you can choose the technique you should employ.

Start each day by being mindful of your thoughts and catching yourself when you are having negative ones.

There are two methods for managing your thoughts:

Technique A: Interrupt and change them
Technique B: Remove them entirely
The second choice is referred to as peace of mind. Your subconscious mind can be reprogrammed using the interrupting and replacing procedure. Over time, the replacement thoughts will take over as the "go-to" thinking in pertinent circumstances.

When dealing with the Inner Critic and Worrier, use Technique A, while when dealing with the Reactor and Sleep Deprived, use Technique B.

1. For the inner critic
When you discover yourself thinking negatively about yourself (beating yourself up, calling yourself names, etc.), stop yourself.
You can mentally shout "Stop! No!" also, "Enough! I'm in charge right now. Then, in place of whatever negative thinking you had about yourself, think

something positive or affirm something that starts with "I am."

You may, for instance, change the idea "I'm such a loser" to "I am a Divine Creation of the Universal Spirit." I am a wonderful spiritual entity growing in my understanding of the human condition. I am an energy, light, and material existence. I am amazing, wise, and lovely. I accept and love myself just as I am.

If you know whose voice it is, you can engage in a debate with yourself to invalidate the "voice" that generated the thought:

"Just because so-and-so called me a loser doesn't necessarily mean that it is true. It wasn't a declaration of fact; it was someone's opinion. Perhaps they were only making fun of me, but I took it seriously because I'm insecure.

You can arrange your counterthoughts or affirmations in advance if you notice that you frequently think of self-critical ideas.

You should forcibly evict this squatter as soon as possible:

They make the Worrier angry.

He also keeps the Reactor present since the names you call yourself turn into triggers when used by other people.

He maintains Sleep Deprived since they are frequently around when you try to get asleep.

They bully others and abuse them verbally and emotionally.

They undermine one's self-worth. They persuade you that you are not deserving. They are lying! Get them out for the sake of your self-worth!

By getting rid of your worst critic, you will also make the other three squatters less noticeable.

Change them out for your new closest pals who will uplift, inspire, and improve your life. You want to have this presence in your head.

2. For the Worrier

Long-term anxiety is unhealthy on mental, emotional, and physical levels. It can affect your health in the long run.

Fear sets off the body's fight-or-flight reaction, worries the mind, and induces anxiety. You could find it more challenging to successfully manage your thoughts as a result.

A "worry thought" should be easy to spot by the way it makes you feel. The following physiological symptoms indicate that the fight-or-flight reaction to fear has begun:

elevated heartbeat, blood pressure, or adrenaline rush

shallow breathing or inability to breathe

tensed muscles

Any worry-related thought should be interrupted using the aforementioned technique, and then replaced. But this time, you'll swap out your worries with feelings of gratitude for the result you've achieved.

This is the perfect time to interact with your higher power if you believe in one. Here's an illustration:

I say the following (I refer to it as a prayer) instead of stressing out about my loved ones traveling in terrible weather:

"I appreciate you, great spirit, keeping watch over. Thank you for keeping an eye on his/her car and ensuring that it is always safe, roadworthy, and free of maintenance difficulties. Thank you for only putting safe, responsible, and attentive drivers around him/her. And I appreciate you keeping him/her safe, responsible, and awake.

When you consider it or say it out loud, smile, and use the present tense. You can feel it and perhaps even start to believe it with the aid of both of these.

If you can picture the outcome of your prayer, the visualization will strengthen your emotions and have a greater impact on your vibrational field.

Take a quiet breath right now, slowly inhaling through your nose and exhaling through your mouth. Take however many you like! Continue doing it until you sense that you are almost in control of your thoughts.

The Reactor will lose steam if fearful thinking patterns are replaced with ones of thankfulness.

For instance, the common parental response after the initial, frightening thoughts of finding your child lost at the mall is to scold them.

"I warned you not to stray from my presence." This response only heightens the child's fear of getting lost.

Additionally, it teaches kids that their parents will get upset if they make a mistake, which could lead them to lie to you or withhold information from you in the future.

When you have scared thoughts, change them:

"I appreciate You (your chosen Higher Power) keeping an eye on my child and keeping him secure. I appreciate your helping me locate him quickly. After going through this process, your sole response will be appreciated when you see your child, which seems like a preferable option for everyone concerned.

3. Concerning the Disruptor, Reactor, or Over-Reactor

It will take a little more time and thought to find and repair the causes of the triggers to permanently remove this intruder. But until then, you can keep the Reactor under control by starting to breathe consciously as soon as you become aware of his presence.

The fight or flight reaction is triggered by the Reactor's thoughts or feelings, just like it is with the Worrier. He will exhibit the same physiological indicators of his presence. You should be able to distinguish between worry, rage, frustration, and pain with a little concentration.

You've probably heard that it's a good idea to count to 10 when you're furious; however, if you are calm, you can use those ten seconds considerably more effectively.

Cognizant breathing is pretty much as straightforward as it sounds — simply be aware of your relaxing. Focus on the air going in and emerging.

Take in through your nose:

Feel the air entering your nose.
Feel your lungs filling and growing.
Center around your midsection rising.
Inhale out through your nose:
Feel your lungs purging.
Center around your gut falling.
Feel the air leaving your nose.
Do this however long you like. Leave what is going on assuming you need. This gives the adrenaline time to standardize. Presently, you can address what is happening with a more settled, more judicious viewpoint and try not to harm conduct, and you'll be more in charge of your viewpoints.

One of the difficulties this vagrant cause is that it adds to the rest depriver's issues. By ousting or

possibly controlling the Reactor, you will diminish the traditionalist way of behaving, which will diminish the requirement for the reiterating and ruminating that might hold you back from nodding off.
Ace your psyche and prevent the Reactor from carrying pressure on you and your connections!

In particular, see your genuine thought process. What's the inward drive that can assist you with continuing to move?

4. For the Sleep deprived
(They're comprised of the Internal Organizer, the Rehasher, and the Ruminator, alongside the Inward Pundit and the Worrier.)

I was tormented with an exceptionally normal issue: not having the option to switch off my brain at sleep time. This powerlessness kept me from nodding off and hence, getting a soothing and supportive night's rest.

This is the way I dominated my brain and removed the Rest Depriver and every one of his colleagues.

I began by zeroing in on my breathing — focusing on the ascent and fall of my midsection — yet that didn't keep the contemplations out for a long time. (All things considered, I presently start by checking my very still mouth position to hold me back from gripping.)
Then, at that point, I thought of a substitution methodology that disposed of uncontrolled reasoning — envisioning the word in while taking in and thinking the word out while breathing out. I would (and do) stretch the word to match the length of my breath.
At the point when I find myself thinking, I shift back to in, out. With this strategy, I'm thinking, kind of, yet the wheels are done going crazy. I'm in charge of my brain and contemplations, and I pick calm.

When I first attempted this strategy, I began to yawn after a couple of cycles and am generally sleeping in ten minutes or less.

For truly troublesome evenings, I add increment consideration by holding my eyes in a looking-into position (shut, obviously). Now and again I attempt to look toward my third eye yet that harms my eyes.

On the off chance that you experience difficulty nodding off because you can't stop your brain, I emphatically suggest you attempt this procedure. I use it consistently. You can begin resting better this evening!

You can likewise utilize this method any time you need to:

Fall back to rest assuming you awaken too early
Close down your reasoning
Quiet your sentiments
Just spotlight on the current second

The Reality

Your brain is a device, and like some other instrument, it tends to be utilized for valuable purposes or damaging purposes.

You can permit your brain to be involved by undesirable, unfortunate, and disastrous inhabitants, or you can pick helpful occupants like harmony, appreciation, sympathy, love, and bliss.

Your psyche can turn into your closest companion, your greatest ally, and somebody you can rely on to be there and empower you. You can be in charge of your viewpoints. The decision is yours!

Chapter 4

How to stop overthinking

Overthinking is the propensity for thinking excessively and additionally too long about something. Overthinking is otherwise called 'examination loss of motion because by thinking an excessive amount you're stalling out in your viewpoints and preventing yourself from making a move.

Sound reasoning, which is praised on World Reasoning Day, opens minds and commends development and strengthening. Yet, overthinking influences the equilibrium into stuckness, weakness, and a psyche that is shut to positive open doors.

However, overthinking is going on all over. Research shows that overthinking is common among youthful (25-35-year-olds) and moderately aged grown-ups (45-55-year-olds). Overthinking will in general be more terrible among ladies. Also, a lot of thinking can prompt psychological wellness issues like wretchedness and uneasiness, profound pain, and pointless ways of behaving.
"Overthinking won't engage you over things that are unchangeable as far as you might be concerned. Thus, let it be if it is intended to be, and value the occasion.

Typical behaviors of an overthinker
There's a running editorial in your mind, scrutinizing and dissecting what you said and did yesterday, unnerved that you look terrible - and worrying about a horrible future that could look for you.
Looking over your choices, froze you've made some unacceptable ones, or delay throughout the following one.

Breaking down what your companion or partner implied by that expendable remark or that sideways look.
Struggling with what to post via web-based entertainment, and concerned when others are making some preferred memories over you, or getting more likes.
Perusing and once again perusing messages to figure out the genuine significance of the message.
'What uncertainties' and 'shoulds' overwhelm your reasoning as though an undetectable jury is sitting in judgment on your life and thinking that it is needed.
Not resting soundly, because all the ruminating and stressing keeps you conscious around evening time.
Feeling misgiving and pummeling yourself for your apparent deficiencies.
In some cases drinking an excess of liquor in a bid to quiet the oppression of your overthinking mind.
Incapable to be consistent with yourself since you're so bustling working out what others need, need, and think.

Understanding the reason why you overthink

There can be many justifications for why one individual overthinks things and another allows life merrily to occur. A portion of the underlying foundations of overthinking can emerge out of early life and encounters with your parental figures.

At the point when you arrived at the formative phase of figuring out how to apply your own will and independence (pre-young), how your folks dealt with you could decide your trust in yourself and your capacities. On the off chance that a parent indulged you and didn't allow you to evaluate new things or have unique contemplations, you might start to be uncertain about your reasoning. Or on the other hand, on the off chance that a parent was excessively basic and caused you to feel deficient at whatever point you made or explored new territory, you might start to be uncertain about your capacity to act. Overthinking keeps you caught in thought without activity.

Your feeling of character might not have been reflected as a youngster. You might have needed to re-think what your folks needed, to stay away from discipline maybe, or to get their consideration. After some time you then, that point, move away from what you need and need and think. Also, you might fear disgrace or embarrassment by accomplishing something openly that might be scrutinized or denounced. That can prompt loss of motion, uncertainty, and a feeling of dread toward setting anything in motion.

Techniques to quit overthinking

If you have any desire to manage your overthinking, there are a few viable procedures to help you:

1. Get out of your head

This is the main cure for overthinking. Anything it removes to get from your head, make it happen. This might be an energetic activity that brings you into your body, a lively stroll in the park, or a movement that doesn't expect you to think excessively. This could be cooking, painting, doing Do-It-Yourself, finishing a jigsaw - anything places you 'in a stream and keeps you loose.

2. Wake up

Track down ways of adjusting to your faculties, with decent things to check out, your number one tunes to pay attention to, a few scented candles to calm you, preparing yourself your #1 food, or having a steaming shower. Deal with your body and give your psyche a break.

3. Be careful

Care procedures can help you reevaluate your contemplations as that: considerations as opposed to realities. They can assist you with slowly bringing down your reasoning and letting contemplations cross your thoughts like mists on a windy day. Care can likewise assist you with being more present in what's going on now, as opposed to projecting into what's to come.

4. Ring-wall your reasoning time

You don't need to completely quit thinking. Yet, rather than permitting your reasoning to spread across your day, diarise some time when you are effectively thinking, pondering, and reflecting.

5. Record your contemplations

Rather than keeping your contemplations in your mind, think of them in a diary or begin a 'considerations container' where you can post your contemplations. Like that, you won't have to clutch them.

6. Pay attention to your instinct

Through every one of the long periods of rethinking others and thinking, reconsidering, and overthinking, you might have overwhelmed your internal voice. You may not understand what it seems like. Paying attention to your instinct might take time and persistence, tuning into your natural sentiments can be an initial step to following up on your terms, as opposed to being caught in an overthinking circle.

7. Speak to a specialist

If overthinking is demolishing your life, and on the off chance that you figure you might be spiraling into a discouraged or restless area in light of your viewpoints, then, at that point, addressing a specialist will uphold you in getting a handle on your reality. Treatment can assist with building your self-personality and make more grounded establishments to empower you to carry on with life now - instead of overthinking a stressful future.

Chapter 5

Positive thinking

(The most effective method to Develop a Positive Outlook)

There is such a lot of material and content around us, rambling fundamental elements of how to be positive to acquire the outcome in life you're pursuing. It's mind-boggling.

You could likewise have become burrow visioned to accept just the mystery tips and guidance endorsed to us by outlook masters at sensationalized gatherings, classes, and meetings that can help us. Such stage instructors appeared to be so clean and ready that it was difficult to oppose that we can change our reasoning without their assistance.

Truly you don't have to forfeit your life investment funds with a mentor to turn your outlook around. With this bit-by-bit guide, you'll understand as of now encapsulate every one of the fixings and the open doors around you to begin developing a positive outlook today. (I'm not denying working with a mentor can help. In any case, you can quick course also a more affordable one!)

Strategies for Developing positive thinking

1. Permit Yourself to Feel Pessimistic Feelings and Quit attempting to be good about everything. It's debilitating, not to mention a ridiculous assumption. Quit paying attention to everybody's recommendation on what you ought to think. Reclaim the reins on concluding how you need to feel about something.

Moreover, you'll begin to be that individual everybody needs to be near. To be positive all the time is attempting to keep yourself from being human. We are brought into the world with the ability to feel a full range of good and pessimistic feelings since they all have worth, significance, and direction for us.

At the point when you permit yourself existence to feel the underlying sting of unsavory feelings, you will find their power decreases and their term abbreviates. Then, at that point, you have more space to begin coordinating your considerations and concentration toward a path that better serves you

.

2. Increase Awareness of Your Current Mindset by Seeking Feedback

Those whose input you trust will be honest and genuinely evenhanded and get some information about what positive and inspiring energy they could encounter just from you being you. Likewise, inquire as to whether they can give instances of how they feel your mentality obstructs you as opposed to helping you.

Asking others for input can be a difficult step. Thusly you're showing you're thinking about a change. Be careful that loved ones can frequently be bulls in a china shop enthusiastically dishing you counsel and analysis from an event that you're not prepared for this, your delicate, delicate profound midsection will turn into a reluctant punching sack.

Recollect that by paying little mind to who you're asking, you're not hoping to request judgment or suppositions. You're requesting that they share with you their perceptions and encounters. The activity is unadulterated to assist you with acquiring uplifted knowledge and picking where you could begin working on making changes.

On the off chance that you in all actuality do feel your criticism sources have misread the activity as a chance to stroke their self-image, condemn you, and lash you with a close-to-home feline o-nine tail, don't fight back or answer. Say thanks to them for their criticism, and park it intellectually into a case that you will return to and survey later.

Your reconsideration likely could be to purge the container essentially! Be that as it may, there additionally may be a trace of validity in the messages they're giving as well.

3. Recognize Unhelpful Thoughts and Language and Practice Reframing Them

Make it a point to yourself mid-sentence and work on reevaluating your words and language. Having the option to get yourself expertise yet you can become deft with training.

Return to the pointless considerations you concocted and check whether you can make slight alterations to the blocking exchange stewing in your mind. "I can't do this" could tenderly turn into "I feel like I can't do this." "That won't ever occur for me" could turn into "it hasn't occurred for me yet".

Focus on the distinction that various words cause you to feel. Notice how various sentences cause you to feel and search for the distinction it makes to how others answer you. Inquiring as to whether you would address a companion or kid in the manner you address yourself can draw fantastic mindfulness of how your language neutralizes you.

It can take a couple of preparing wheel meetings with a mentor or specialist to assist you with creating reevaluating methods. Applying them long enough for you to begin feeling and seeing a distinction. The venture is justified. The advantage of this expertise not just charges your positive outlook; it affects people around you.

4. Cautiously Pick Circumstances to Sow the Seeds of Your Positive Outlook

Keep it easy, to begin with. Just pick a couple of settings in your day-to-day existence where you believe you could rehearse a more sure way of behaving or potentially language changes. However, pick carefully. Be mindful to try not to begin with circumstances where you feel - or have been told - you ought to.

Ought to is a word weighted with assumption. It likewise suggests you want reclamation since you settled on a lower-gave decision in any case. You understood what you could do, be or say and you decided not to. That is weighty stuff! It's not the most ideal beginning stage to have a go at developing a positive outlook. Attempting to create from circumstances discolored with the stamp of censure generally feels harder.

Try not to attempt to make an enormous mentality circle back in a short space of time. You'll probably be met with causing a stir and a name of being inauthentic. Not being irritated when your mother by marriage comes around unannounced and stays for a long time once more, maybe too enormous an outlook challenge to begin with.

Like a tree seedling needs a groundwork of good soil for it to have a battling opportunity, an unbiased circumstance will give you a strong groundwork to rehearse and develop your positive outlook. Consider what is happening that is probably going to rehash the same thing in your regular daily existence:

Welcoming individuals at work when you show up.
Getting your espresso at the equivalent bistro every morning en route to work.
You and your accomplice's morning schedule before you both head separate ways of making money.
Pick settings where you are sincerely and intellectually uninterested and where you could - not ought to - test straightforward ways of behaving or language changes. You're searching for quiet consistent waters you can head out on to test new certain attitude methodologies, and afterward see

how individuals answer your changes, without tension and assumption.

5. Analyze the Positive mindset of Individuals You Appreciate yet Put forth Your Objectives

Presently you've picked your setting to begin rehearsing transforms, you currently need to conclude what changes you will make.

Conceptualizing potential outcomes can be trying from your ongoing attitude. Simplify it. Look outside yourself for pieces of information and ideas. Whose books infuse energy into your spirit through their composed words? Whose TED talks, meets, and digital recordings settle on your gesture in understanding? Who has motivated you to essentially make arrangements to make a move toward doing or being what you have been for a long time needed to do? Who are those individuals? What is it about them that impacts you emphatically?

Concentrate on them. Notice their way of behaving, their language, and how they answer misfortunes and affliction. Watch them intently. Presently contrast how they manage how you ordinarily respond in comparative circumstances.

The correlation is to assist you with checking what changes you want to aim for in your conduct, your correspondence, and your reasoning. Keep in mind, you are not hoping to duplicate these individuals. The world necessities the best of you not a duplicate of Oprah, Tony Robbins, or Jack Canfield! Furthermore, there would not be anything more bothering than seeing a profoundly regarded industry master's protégé begin dressing the same way, attempting to call everybody 'buddy' because the master tends to their confided in staff along these lines.

Individuals see through copycats. They are inauthentic and exhausting, best-case scenario!

Taking the case of your hello individuals in the first part of the day when you show up at your working environment, your ongoing beginning to the day might spread out as follows:

- You don't recognize or converse with anybody in the lift.
- You say 'howdy' to the assistant, Anna, in transit to your work area.

- You mechanically say 'Hey Mary, how are you?' to your associate without seeing her, put your sacks down, put your suit coat on the rear of your seat and turn on your PC.
- You murmur as you sit and contemplate internally: 'Same thing, different day; oh well, business as usual.'

Presently, if you somehow happened to put an Oprah-like twist on this equivalent circumstance, what changes could you hold back nothing? What could feel generally normal to you? What changes in your way of behaving, correspondence, and thinking might you at any point establish here?

Chapter 6

The path to self-acceptance

An absence of self-acceptance can keep you down in each part of your life. It influences your certainty and can keep you from arriving at your maximum capacity.

Individuals with high self-acceptance are stronger in analysis. They comprehend that tolerant themselves while additionally working for ceaseless personal development is OK.

In any case, what is self-acceptance? Also, for what reason are certain individuals more self-tolerating than others? What might it do for you, and how might you develop a greater amount of it? We should figure it out

What is self-acceptance

Self-acceptance is the demonstration of tolerating yourself and all your character attributes precisely as they are. You acknowledge them regardless of whether they are positive or negative. This incorporates your physical and mental qualities.

Self-acceptance implies perceiving that your worth goes past your characteristics and activities. This is here and there known as extremist self-acceptance. self-acceptance gives you more trust in yourself and makes you less defenseless against analysis. It means to profoundly and acknowledge each part of yourself genuinely and no matter what.

To accomplish self-acceptance, you should figure out how to acknowledge the pieces of yourself you think about negative or unwanted.

It's likewise vital to recognize and commend your positive characteristics and accomplishments. Surveying your objectives and your advancement on them helps you to remember your assets.

This is the reason so many of us battle with self-acceptance. We will generally stow away, disregard, and reject the pieces of ourselves we consider unsatisfactory. We would prefer to transform them than acknowledge them.

Even though it could appear to be unreasonable, absolute self-acceptance can assist us with changing the parts of ourselves that we may be less partial to. Having a familiarity with our limits is the initial step on the way to self-awareness and is an indication of the capacity to understand individuals on a deeper level.

Self-acceptance doesn't simply mean tolerating our negative characteristics and abandoning evolving them.
Running against the norm implies monitoring our shortcomings without having any profound connection to them. This mindfulness can assist us with working on our way of behaving and assembling better propensities.

How does self-acceptance influence your everyday life?

Research shows that self-acceptance is essential for general emotional wellness and prosperity. The proof appears to show an immediate connection between low degrees of self-acceptance and dysfunctional behavior.
In any case, there are alternate ways that low self-acknowledgment influences your day-to-day existence, work, connections, and prosperity. The following are five models;

1. Self-acceptance assists you with controlling your feelings.

An absence of self-acceptance can influence the piece of your mind liable for controlling your feelings. This can prompt mental irregularity and close-to-home eruptions because of raised nervousness, stress, or outrage.

An absence of self-acceptance restricts your ability for satisfaction. It likewise influences your mental and close-to-home prosperity. It keeps you zeroed in on the pessimistic parts of yourself, and these pessimistic considerations make gloomy feelings. On the other hand, elevated degrees of self-acknowledgment are connected to additional positive feelings and more noteworthy mental prosperity. Self-acceptance can support your mindset and safeguard you from the impacts of pressure and misery.

2. Self-acceptance assists you with excusing yourself.

Figuring out how to acknowledge yourself assists you with being less self-basic. It assists you with making a more sure, sympathetic, and adjusted perspective on yourself. the powerlessness to acknowledge and pardon ourselves makes us split into various parts.

These two sections — the one that should be excused and the one that requirements to pardon — are in conflict with each other. Self-acceptance can assist you with overcoming any barrier between them, empowering you to excuse yourself for your missteps and continue.

This is fundamental for your prosperity, as choosing not to move on will keep you caught in the pattern of pessimistic contemplations and feelings.

3. Self-acceptance gives you more fearlessness

Self-acceptance can give you more trust in yourself. It assists you with the understanding that your apparent negative characteristics don't characterize you or your value.

At the point when you are sure, you are bound to make a move notwithstanding your feelings of dread. Interestingly, an absence of self-acknowledgment can keep you down and prevent you from pursuing your fantasies.

Self-acceptance assists you with the understanding that disappointment doesn't characterize you and is consistently a learning and an open door on the way to progress.

Certainty can likewise give you more noteworthy freedom. It permits you to settle on choices for yourself without requiring the endorsement of others.

4. Self-acceptance assists you with acting naturally

At the point when you need self-acceptance, you're continually attempting to stow away, control, or quell your actual self. This can leave you feeling depleted.

Self-acceptance can assist you with appearing all the more legitimately without stressing over others' decisions of you. When you acknowledge yourself, you go ahead and be your entire self.

What drives self-acceptance?

Certain individuals are normally more self-tolerating than others. Have you at any point asked why that is? This is because our life as a youngster encounters influence our degrees of self-acceptance as grown-ups.

Our folks or guardians are the initial ones to show us which parts of us are OK and which aren't.

As youngsters, we learn just to acknowledge the pieces of ourselves that they consider adequate. We judge different pieces of ourselves as off-base, and we reject, stifle, and attempt to conceal them.

However, the issue is that these decisions are erratic. They rely upon the qualities and needs of your folks or parental figures.
For instance, various feelings are viewed as OK in various families. If you experienced childhood in a family in which outrage was unsuitable, you may not be able to acknowledge the pieces of yourself that vibe outrage or fury.
The nurturing style likewise assumes a part in your degrees of self-acceptance. Youngsters accept each analysis their folks level them and acknowledge them as truth.
So on the off chance that your folks were exceptionally basic or requesting, the voice of your inward pundit will probably have serious areas of strength for being, and you may likewise have a feeling of dread toward disappointment. Then again, those with additional sympathetic guardians will quite often show more sympathy toward themselves.

Youngsters likewise don't have the foggiest idea how to recognize their way of behaving and themselves. That's what they imagine assuming their way of behaving is inadmissible, which implies they are likewise unsuitable.

In this manner, individuals whose guardians were basic are bound to battle with self-acceptance.

Individuals whose guardians were more certain and attesting are bound to have more elevated levels of self-acceptance.

What is my degree of self-acceptance?

You most likely know whether your degree of self-acceptance is high or low. In any case, to get a thought, recall your young life.

Were your folks or essential parental figures negative and basic? Did they zero in on their analysis of you as an individual as opposed to your way of behaving?

Assuming you responded yes to these inquiries, there's a decent opportunity that your self-acknowledgment is low.

The following is a rundown of signs that you might be inadequate about self-acknowledgment:

You experience issues recognizing and discussing your disappointments, shortcomings, and negative characteristics.

You need self-esteem and genuinely want to be somebody other than what your identity is.

Your point of view is negative for not a glaringly obvious explanation.

You will generally be exacting of yourself and uncertain of your character.

Assuming you routinely experience at least one of these signs, you probably have low self-acceptance. Reflection and other care practices can assist you with building your self-acceptance after some time. This, thusly, will further develop your psychological and close-to-home prosperity.

Let's take a look at five exercises you can do daily to build self-acceptance.

Five self-acceptance exercises

Genuine self-acceptance doesn't simply work out coincidentally. Everyday practice and taking care of oneself can assist you with bit by bit expanding your degree of self-acceptance over the long run.

These self-acceptance activities will show you how to rehearse confidence and acknowledgment consistently:

1. Practice appreciation

Consistently, record three to five things you're appreciative of. This can appear to be trying from

the get-go, particularly when you have a psychological propensity for zeroing in on the negative.
In any case, rehearsing appreciation consistently can assist you with retraining your cerebrum to zero in on the positive.
Search for the silver linings of every regrettable circumstance. Assuming you fizzled at something, be thankful for the illustrations learned. Search for things about your apparent blemishes to be thankful for, as well.

2. Re-evaluate your negative thought
Negative convictions are the voice of your internal pundit. They cause a ton of misery and keep you from arriving at unqualified self-acknowledgment.

Rethink your negative convictions about yourself by thinking of them down. For instance, on the off chance that you accept you are a terrible individual for something you did before, get it on paper.

Whenever you've composed your rundown, go through every conviction and reevaluate it. Begin by testing every assertion by asking yourself: "Is this valid?"

Then, supplant every assertion with more certain self-talk. For instance: "I'm a decent individual, yet I'm just human, so I in some cases commit errors."

3. Pick your emotionally supportive network

Cause a rundown of individuals you invest the most energy with. Contemplate how they address you — would they say they are for the most part sure or negative?

Distinguish the individuals who are generally negative and inquire as to whether investing less energy with them would be conceivable. Maybe you might kill them from your life.

This isn't generally imaginable, like in that frame of mind of a nearby relative. Be that as it may, attempt to eliminate whatever number of gloomy individuals from your life as could be expected under the circumstances. Encircle yourself with positive individuals who value you and lift you.

4. MEDITATE

Standard meditation practice can assist you with isolating yourself from your negative self-talk. This can work on your temperament and lead to additional positive feelings.

The objective of meditation is to become mindful of those considerations, noticing them without relating to them.

Care rehearses, for example, reflection increases mental prosperity.

This assists you with diminishing self-analysis and working on your mental self-view.

5. FORGIVE YOURSELF

Mercy for previous oversights and second thoughts is a fundamental stage toward self-acknowledgment. Utilize this self-absolution exercise to beat previous slip-ups. It will advise you that you're just human and that you did all that could be expected. This will assist you with relinquishing misgiving and continuing.

Consider what is happening, and what activity, or what mix-up for which you might want to excuse yourself. Recognize any decisions of yourself connecting with that particular situation, and get them on paper.

For instance, you could state, "I shouldn't have done X. I'm so inept."

Then, pardon yourself for that conviction. Record something like: "I pardon myself for accepting I'm moronic for that. Truly… " and fill in the clear. Contemplate what an empathetic companion could share with you. It very well may be a like thing, "I was focused on because… " or "I was harming and settled on a terrible choice."

Let radical self-acceptance empower you

To acknowledge yourself is to step into your power. At the point when you develop self-acceptance, you never again need to search for outer wellsprings of approval. Figuring out how to acknowledge yourself is a venturing stone to how you deal with your psychological wellness, as well.

You become sure of what your identity is and figure out how to possess both your assets and your shortcomings.

Chapter 7

Practice radical self-love

We often think about giving our love to
We frequently contemplate giving our affection to other people, however, when did you last ponder cherishing yourself?

At the end of the day, truly, inquire as to whether you even understand what confidence truly is. Without a doubt, you can say OK, giving yourself significance and focusing on your tranquility and well-being over different responsibilities. In any case, is that it? Is that all confidence is? What's more, doesn't it sound a great deal like being childish to put ourselves before others? Such countless inquiries, correct?

What is self-love?

At the point when we consider self-love, we frequently consider it thought of cherishing yourself

and focusing on yourself over others. Yet, there is something else to self-love besides that.
Adoring ourselves comprises performing such activities and remembering to help our development genuinely, profoundly, intellectually, and inwardly. It is purposefully integrating propensities into your life to deal with your necessities and sustain them to empower your development in all parts of life. Simultaneously, self-love likewise expects us to abstain from forfeiting our prosperity to attempt to satisfy others. By cherishing yourself, you really can all the more effectively express love towards others. One normal inquiry that generally rings a bell is how self-love is not the same as being selfish. All things considered, self-love incorporates focusing on one's self over others. While there are most certainly egotistical, undesirable types of self-love, not all types of self-love are unfortunate.

So that makes one wonder, what is healthy self-love?

What are instances of solid self-love?
First of all, it tends to be:

- Favoring genuineness over beguile.
- Not needing a single thing from others except for their adoration and kinship.
- Being legitimately you, regardless of whether it might harm your standing.
- Regarding others as significant in their privileges however not allowing them to exploit you.
- Finding opportunities to pay attention to others from varying backgrounds yet knowing when to recharge.
- Defining solid limits.
- Excusing yourself when you are not being great or certifiable to yourself.
- Focusing on your very own ventures over the requests of others.
- Grant yourself to have a good time

For what reason is self-love so significant?

We should check a couple of models out. I was perusing the narrative of a 24-year-elderly person named Ruth who was in a scathing four-year relationship that underestimated her objectives and goals. Through this experience and separation, she understood the significance of self-esteem.

According to Ruth, "I, before, frequently recognized my loved ones accomplishments by underestimating mine. My viewpoint in focusing on myself was so misshaped I saw my achievements as 'humble' and continually contrasted myself with others. I'm currently discovering that isn't correct confidence.

Cherishing myself makes everybody around me more significant because I perceive the value independently, preliminaries, and accomplishments and value my endeavors to battle for me and be a superior entire being. I'm not generally separated by correlations since I generally pick me."
Then there is Mary, who needed to drastically completely change herself in the wake of going through a critical well-being alarm prompting a kidney relocate.

Mary makes sense of, "That implied leaving a profession that I felt characterized me and tolerating that I needed to modify my life and rely upon others interestingly. I was lost and frightened. On one occasion my specialist asked me how I was doing myself. I was confused! I understood that I wasn't doing anything for myself.

I started to cut out minutes that gave me delight from that day forward. I began with small steps. A nail treatment. A stroll with my canine. Losing all sense of direction in an extraordinary book. I've presently arrived where I'm making a move to investigate an everyday routine that I've for a long time needed to experience and never felt commendable or free enough to have. I'm so thankful for the straightforward inquiry that was posed to me quite a while back. It's begun me on a whole excursion through my effort."

These accounts represent that the force of self-love is more critical than some other part of our life — all things considered, in this body, you will lie, and in this body, you will kick the bucket. You will encounter all sorts of challenges, come what may.

What's more, it's not generally a simple way. Self-love requires sound selfishness, which is established in persistence, empathy, and figuring out how to develop and be blissful.

It is understanding that you can't make any other person cheerful except if you find a sense of contentment with yourself, and for that, confidence is fundamental. That is a general purpose.

How do you learn self-love?

Accept your feelings

We frequently end up taking off from what we feel, particularly notwithstanding gloomy feelings. This is a steady deterrent to accomplishing self-love. In this way, the initial step is to acknowledge what you feel and be alright with it. Try not to discredit your feelings and considerations.

Quit constraining yourself to be perfect.

The consistent desire and strain to be the absolute best individual can be a genuine obstacle in one's excursion toward accomplishing confidence. Quit being so cruel to yourself and quit believing that you are worthless without flawlessness.

Embrace the uncertainty.

We frequently beat ourselves over things that have occurred in the past without understanding that a few things are beyond our control, and regardless of the amount we ponder them, we can't transform them. Give up and acknowledge the void.

Why is self-love so tricky?

While it's not difficult to expand love and sympathy toward others, communicating adoration and empathy for ourselves can be significantly more tested. That is because internal harmony and joy are inseparable from developing sympathy toward ourselves, which is easy to talk about, but not so easy to do.

Self-love and internal harmony are something beyond indulging ourselves with a long walk, getting a back rub, or cleaning up before bed. Albeit these things could help, self-love is internal work. It has to do with self-empathy in treating ourselves and connecting with our feelings.

It implies purposefully tracking down the strength and versatility to embrace the full scope of the human feelings that we experience. It's tied in with searching internally so we invite our sentiments as opposed to defying them with self-hatred or decisions. Being human means grappling with awkward feelings and tolerating and adoring yourself how you are.

Habits that encourage self-love

No momentous accomplishment is accomplished without embracing specific positive propensities. Likewise, self-esteem additionally requests the advancement of such practices that empower it. We should get into the absolute best propensities:

Carve out time for yourself.

That sounds incomprehensible, correct? Since you are excessively occupied? Excessively occupied to deal with yourself? That appears to be somewhat uncalled for, right? Sure work is fundamental, and it isn't generally imaginable to require heaps of investment for ourselves in this way, it is reasonable for you to begin little. Begin by requiring 15-30 minutes and working on something for yourself. That could be anything from perusing a book, having some espresso, taking a walk, journaling, or working out.

Deal with your actual well-being.
Dealing with your body is one of the most basic parts of self-love. What better method for having a decent outlook on yourself than keeping your body in shape? Make a propensity for practicing consistently to deliver pressure and yet again charge your energy.

Choose your company carefully.
Confidence expects that you require some investment to sit alone and find a sense of contentment with your viewpoints. It very well may be testing on the off chance that people around you don't have comprehension and a steady demeanor. Relinquish the pessimistic impacts and encircle yourself with individuals who make you a superior variant of yourself. Our company essentially affects us, so invest your energy with your loved ones. This will make your excursion of self-love a lot more straightforward.

Become careful to quit corrupting yourself.
Let yourself know day to day that you can accomplish anything you desire, at whatever point you need it. Begin the act of journaling three things every day that you are delighted in getting.

Don't compare yourself with others.
Be happy with what you have and quit imagining that you rival somebody.

Final thought
The significance of self-love is huge because main through adoring ourselves could we at any point love others and get positive changes in others' lives. Self-love is critical to tracking down satisfaction and making significant progress in each part of life.

Individuals who have a charitable and cherishing direction toward others will generally encourage that same light. This capacity to focus on affection is made conceivable, to a great extent, by the ability to quiet the self-image.

Keep in mind, there never has been, nor will there at any point be a solitary individual who at any point lived on this planet that was you. You are one of a kind. This uniqueness is your superpower. Try not to squander it. Live deliberately and begin praising yourself.

"In these bodies, we will live; in these bodies, we will pass on. Where you contribute your adoration, you contribute your life."

www.ingramcontent.com/pod-product-compliance
Lightning Source LLC
LaVergne TN
LVHW052051160826
845678LV00015B/3173

* 9 7 9 8 3 5 7 4 4 2 2 8 4 *